101 Lessons from

The Bhagvad Gita

Timeless teachings & Purpose

Noor Paintal Baruta

Made with ❤ on the Notion Press Platform
www.notionpress.com

Introduction: The Timeless Beauty of The Bhagavad Gita

The Bhagavad Gita is more than a scripture; it is a timeless guide to the art of living. Spoken amidst the battlefield of life, its wisdom transcends centuries, offering answers to humanity's most profound questions: Who am I? Why am I here? How can I find peace in a world of chaos?

This sacred dialogue between Lord Krishna and Arjuna is a treasure trove of insights that beautifully intertwine philosophy, spirituality, and practicality. The Gita doesn't demand blind faith; it invites you to explore, reflect, and realize the profound truths of existence. It speaks to the seeker in all of us, whether we are overwhelmed by choices, weighed down by challenges, or simply searching for meaning and joy.

The beauty of The Bhagvad Gita lies in its universal relevance. Its teachings are not bound by religion, culture, or era. They illuminate the path of self-awareness, urging us to embrace our strengths, overcome our fears, and rise above the illusions of ego and attachment. The Gita reveals that life is not a random series of events but a divine journey where each moment offers an opportunity to grow, love, and connect with the infinite.

To truly understand the Gita is to unlock the door to inner peace. Its teachings guide us to live in harmony with ourselves and the world, cultivating a sense of contentment that is unshaken by external circumstances. By walking this path, we transform not only our lives but also the lives of those around us, becoming a source of light and positivity.

May this book be your companion on the path to self-discovery, a source of wisdom in moments of doubt, and a reminder that the journey to joy and peace begins within.

As Krishna promises in The Bhagvad Gita, "When a man finds joy in the self and the self alone, he finds true peace."

To my children,

I hope this book helps you navigate through the difficult times in your lives, through moments of disappointments and times when nothing seems to be working.

I hope you find a chapter from this book to answer your questions everytime you are lost or afraid.

I hope you live your lives with compassion, gratitude and contentment.

I hope you always have it in you to forgive others and find peace from within.

Love,
Mom

Chapter1: Embracing Your True Essence

"Knowing yourself is the beginning of all wisdom."
Aristotle

The Bhagavad Gita begins by urging us to discover our true essence. You are not merely this body or mind; you are the eternal, indestructible soul. Recognizing this liberates you from the fleeting highs and lows of worldly life.

Understating yourself goes beyond introspection. It is anbout aligning with your divine essence. This realization helps you live with purpose and inner peace, free from the need for external validation.

From a psychological viewpoint, unveiling the true self involves discovering and embracing your authentic identity, free from societal expectations, external influences, and internal fears.

Practice: Spend five minutes in self-reflection daily. Ask yourself, "Who am I beyond my labels and roles?" Journal your thoughts to deepen this awareness. Nourish your soul with deeper experiences because the soul is eternal and indestructible.

When Arjuna is overcome with sorrow for fighting and killing his own kin on the battlefield, Lord Krishna explains that our true essence is the Atman (soul). It is eternal, unchanging and your pure self (your essence) that is beyond the ego, mind and body.

"As the embodied soul continuously passes, in this body, from boyhood to youth to old age, the soul similarly passes into another body at death. The wise are not deluded by this."
(Bhagavad Gita 2.13)

When you realize that you are the self and not your roles, emotions, or attachments, you rise above fear, grief, and confusion.

Your essence does not age, suffer, or die. It is only the body that changes.

Chapter 2: The mind: Friend or Foe

"You have power over your mind, not outside events.
Realize this, and you will find strength."
Marcus Aurelius

The Bhagavad Gita warns that an undisciplined mind is your greatest enemy, while a controlled mind becomes your most loyal ally. Mastery over your thoughts is the key to lasting peace.

An uncontrolled mind fuels confusion, fear, and impulsive decisions. By calming the mental chatter, you unlock wisdom, resilience, and clarity in every situation.

Practice: Whenever your mind feels unsettled, pause and take ten slow, deep breaths. Focus on a calming phrase like, "I am at peace."

Whilst on the battlefield of Mahabharata, a troubled
Arjuna asks Lord Krishna,
"O Krishna, you speak of yoga and self-realization.
How can I walk this path when my own mind is my
enemy? It is restless and stubborn. Controlling it feels
harder than catching the wind itself."

Krishna smiles and responds,
"Yes, Arjuna, the mind is undoubtedly very restless,
but it can be brought under control. Through constant
practice (abhyasa) and detachment (vairagya), even the
wildest mind can become still."

He adds "A person must uplift themselves with their
own mind, not degrade themselves by it. The mind can
be your best friend or your greatest enemy."

Arjuna, gaining some clarity respond
"So the real battle begins within."

Krishna nodded
"Always, my friend."

Chapter 3: Detaching From Results

"Do your work with your whole heart, and you will succeed, there's so little competition."
Elbert Hubbard

The Bhagavad Gita teaches that attachment to results binds us to anxiety. Instead, focus on giving your best and trust that the outcome will take care of itself. Detachment isn't indifference, it is about staying centered amidst success and failure.

When Arjuna is hesitant to fight in the war, Krishna reminds him to rise above personal attachments and focus on his dharma (duty as a warrior). Krishna says, "You have a right to perform your actions, but not to the fruits of those actions."
(Bhagvad Gita 2.47)

This means one should act sincerely and wholeheartedly without being emotionally attached to success or failure. He emphasiszes that attachment to results brings anxiety and disappointment, while detachment leads to peace, focus, and spiritual growth.

Krishna advises Arjuna to treat success and failure alike. This mindset purifies the soul and leads to liberation.

Practice: While working on a task, repeat to yourself, "I dedicate this effort to a higher purpose." Let the process itself bring you joy.

Chapter 4: Dharma- Your Unique Path

"Everyone has his own specific vocation or mission in life."
Viktor E. Frankl

In The Bhagavad Gita, dharma is your sacred duty. It isthe unique role you are meant to fulfill. Aligning with it brings meaning and peace to your life.

Following your dharma requires courage, as it often challenges societal expectations. But living authentically creates harmony within and around you.

Practice: Identify one aspect of your life where you feel a sense of purpose. Take a small step today to honor and nurture it.

As the Mahabharata war is about to begin, Arjuna is
heartbroken to see his family, teachers, and friends on
both sides of the battlefield.

Arjuna asks Lord Krishna,
"How can I kill my own family, Krishna?
They are my teachers, my cousins, my loved ones.
What good can come from such a war, even if we win?
I'd rather be killed unarmed than raise my weapon
against them."
(Bhagavad Gita Chapter 1, Verses 28–39)

Krishna responds with wisdom and clarity,
"As a warrior, your dharma is to fight for righteousness.
To abandon it out of fear or attachment is dishonor."
(Bhagvad Gita 2.31–33)

Lord Krishna teaches that even when it is the most
difficult thing to do, one must follow their duty.

Chapter 5: Actions Speak Louder Than Words

""Well done is better than well said."
Benjamin Frankli

The Bhagavad Gita emphasizes that spirituality is reflected in your actions, not just in words or rituals. Let your deeds align with your values.

Your true character is revealed through how you treat others and navigate challenges. Consistent, meaningful actions inspire and uplift those around you.

Practice: Perform one selfless act today without expecting recognition. Let your action embody kindness and integrity.

As Arjuna begins to understand the importance of
inner realization, he asks Lord Krishna,
"O Krishna, if knowledge is greater than action, then
why do you urge me to engage in this terrible act of
war? Wouldn't it be better to renounce all action and
choose quiet wisdom?"
(Bhagavad Gita, Chapter 3, Verse 1)

Krishna replies,
"Set an example with your actions, not just your
words. The wise lead by doing, so that others may
follow."
(Bhagvad Gita 3.21)

Chapter 6: Conquer Desire, Conquer Suffering

"He who is not contented with what he has would not be contented with what he would like to have." Socrates

The Bhagavad Gita teaches that unchecked desires lead to restlessness and suffering. Contentment arises when you master your cravings rather than letting them master you.

Desires aren't inherently bad, but clinging to them disrupts your peace. Learn to appreciate what you have, and desires will no longer control you.

Practice: When tempted by a desire, pause and ask, "Will this truly bring me lasting happiness?" Shift your focus to gratitude for what you already have.

Arjuna, trying to understand what makes people act
against their own values and fall into destructive
behavior asks Lord Krishna,
"O Krishna, what is it that drives a person to commit
wrong, even unwillingly, as if forced by some unseen
power?"
(Bhagavad Gita Chapter 3, Verse 36)

Lord Krishna replies,
"It is desire, born of passion, that becomes anger
when unfulfilled. It is the great devourer, the enemy of
the wise. Desire clouds wisdom and hides the truth.
Conquer desire by mastering the senses and mind.
When you control desire, you rise above suffering and
reach peace."
(Bhagvad Gita 3.37- 3.43)

Chapter 7: Balance is The Key to Harmony

"Happiness is not a matter of intensity but of balance, order, rhythm, and harmony."
Thomas Merton

In The Bhagavad Gita, Krishna advises moderation in all aspects of life- work, rest, and recreation. Extremes lead to instability, while balance fosters well-being.

A balanced life nurtures both your body and spirit. Strive for equilibrium, and you'll find energy, focus, and joy in your daily pursuits.

Practice: Identify one area of excess in your life, be it overworking, overeating, or oversleeping. Make one adjustment today to restore balance.

As Arjuna grows spiritually, he wonders how a person can live a disciplined life without being an extremist.
He asks Lord Krishna,
"O Krishna, is the path of yoga only for those who completely renounce pleasures and live in extreme discipline? How can a balanced life lead to peace?"
(Bhagavad Gita Chapter 6, Verse 16)

Krishna replies,
"No, Arjuna. The path of yoga is not for one who eats too much or too little, sleeps too much or too little.
But for one who is balanced in eating, sleeping, working, and recreation. Such a person finds peace and freedom from suffering. Balance is the key to harmony."
(Bhagvad Gita 6.16- 6.18)

A life of balance leads to peace, clarity, and inner freedom.

Chapter 8: Be Like a Lotus

"You can't stop the waves, but you can learn to surf."
Jon Kabat-Zinn

The Bhagavad Gita uses the lotus as a symbol of purity and detachment. It thrives in muddy water but remains untouched by it.

Living like the lotus means engaging with the world while staying rooted in your values. External negativity won't disturb you when your inner self is steady.

Practice: Visualize yourself as a lotus during a challenging moment. Rise above the situation with grace and clarity.

Arjuna, trying to understand how to live in the
world without being trapped by it, asks Lord
Krishna,
"Krishna, how can a person stay detached while
performing duties in this world full of desires and
attachments?"
(Bhagavad Gita Chapter 5, Verse 10)

Lord Krishna replied,
"One who performs their duties without
attachment, offering all actions to the Divine,
remains untouched by sin- just as a lotus remains
untouched by water."
(Bhagavad Gita 5.10)

The lotus grows in muddy water but stays pure and
untouched by it. In the same way, a wise person
lives in the world, doing their duties, yet remains
inwardly free and unaffected by success, failure,
praise, or blame"

"Be in the world, but not of it, like a lotus that
blooms in water yet remains untouched by it."

Chapter 9: The Essence of Freewill

"Uddhared atmanatmanam, natmanam avasadayet.
Atmaiva hy atmano bandhuh, atmaiva ripur atmanah."
(Bhagavad Gita 6.5)

"One must elevate oneself by one's own mind, not degrade oneself. The mind is the friend of the conditioned soul, and it is also the enemy."

The Bhagavad Gita emphasizes that freewill lies in our ability to choose our thoughts and actions. While external circumstances may be beyond our control, we have the power to shape our inner world. By aligning our choices with dharma (righteousness) and cultivating self-awareness, we can elevate ourselves.

Misuse of freewill, driven by ignorance or desire, leads to self-destruction, making the mind an enemy.

The Bhagvad Gita thus teaches that freewill is a tool given to humans to transcend the limitations of the ego and move closer to self-realization. We are guided, but our choices shape our path.

Practice: By practicing conscious decision-making daily, you transform freewill into a pathway to inner harmony and spiritual growth.

As Krishna explains duty and the soul, Arjuna wonders if we truly have free will or is everything driven by fate and divine will.

He asks Lord Krishna,
"O Krishna, after all that you've taught me about action, duty, and surrender, do I truly have the freedom to choose? Or is everything predetermined?"
(Bhagvad Gita Chapter 18, Verse 63)

Lord Krishna replies,
"I have explained to you the most sacred knowledge. Now, reflect on it fully. Then do as you wish."
(Bhagavad Gita 18.63)

Chapter 10: Anger Can be Constructive

"For every minute you remain angry, you give up sixty seconds of peace of mind."
Ralph Waldo Emerson

The Bhagavad Gita teaches that anger clouds judgment and leads to harm. Patience and self-awareness are the keys to mastering this powerful emotion. It teaches that anger, if left unchecked, leads to destruction. But when channeled constructively, it becomes a force for positive change.

Anger is a signal, not a solution. By responding thoughtfully instead of reacting impulsively, you transform challenges into opportunities for growth.

According to mental health professionals, Anger is normal and can be helpful when handled well. Experts suggest recognizing your anger, pausing to understanding it, expressing it calmly and using it to solve problems or set boundaries.

Practice: Instead of reacting impulsively, use anger as a signal to pause, reflect, and choose a response that aligns with your values and long-term goals.

Arjuna, troubled by emotions like anger clouding his clarity, questions Lord Krishna,
"Why do emotions like anger overpower our intentions?"
(Bhagavad Gita 3.36)

Lord Krishna empathetic, as always, answers,
"It is desire, Arjuna. From desire arises anger, when desires are unfulfilled. and from anger comes delusion, delusion leads to loss of memory, memory loss destroys discrimination and with that, the self is lost."
(Bhagvad Gita 2.62–63, 3.37)

"But he who masters desire and anger, through self-discipline and wisdom, becomes steady and peaceful."
(Bhagvad Gita 3.43)

Chapter 11: The Power of Now

"Do not dwell in the past, do not dream of the future, concentrate the mind on the present moment."
Buddha

The Bhagavad Gita reminds us that life unfolds in the present. Dwelling on the past or worrying about the future robs us of the richness of the now.

Being present allows you to fully experience life as it is, without regret or anxiety. The present is where you find peace, joy, and purpose.

"Realize deeply that the present moment is all you ever have. Make the Now the primary focus of your life."
-Ekhart Tolle, The Power of Now

Tolle emphasizes that the mind often dwells in the past or projects into the future, causing unnecessary suffering through regret, anxiety, and fear. However, the present moment the "Now" is the only reality. By anchoring yourself in the present, you can break free from mental chatter and fully experience life with clarity, peace, and joy.

Practice: When distracted, take three deep breaths and focus on what you see, hear, and feel around you. Anchor yourself in the moment.

Trying to seek clarity on how one can attain lasting
peace and wisdom while focusing on their dharma,
Arjuna asks Lord Krishna,
"Krishna, how can I rise above confusion and gain true
peace in the middle of all this chaos?"
(Bhagvad Gita, Chapter 4 Verse 38)

Lord Krishna, often teaching Arjuna that awakening,
clarity and peace come from being fully present and
detached from past and future, replies,
"In this world, there is nothing as purifying as true
knowledge. One who is perfected in yoga finds this
truth within. In time, and with a mind focused in the
present."
(Bhagvad Gita 4.38)

He emphasises time and again that when the mind is
rooted in the now, wisdom shines like the sun through
the fog.

Most pain comes from ruminating about the past or
worrying about the future. Being present eliminates
these patterns.

Chapter 12: Rise Above Dualities

"Success is not final, failure is not fatal: it is the courage to continue that counts."
Winston Churchill

The Bhagavad Gita teaches that life is full of dualities, joy and sorrow, success and failure. Rising above them brings equanimity and peace.

Arjuna's situation in the Mahabharata is anstrong reminder that opposites are inevitable in life. Peace comes from not being moved by them, but by accepting them with equanimity.

True strength lies in accepting life's contrasts without being swayed. This balanced approach helps you remain grounded through all seasons of life.

Practice: When faced with a challenge, remind yourself, "After the hardships, easy times will follow."

Arjuna is overwhelmed by opposing emotions- love
and duty, joy and sorrow, gain and loss. He seeks
Lord Krishna's wisdom on how to handle the
conflicting emotions,

Confused, he asks Lord Krishna,
"Krishna, how can one remain peaceful in a world
full of opposites- like pleasure and pain, success and
failure?"
(Bhagvad Gita, Chapter 2)

Lord Krishna responds calmly,
"O son of Kunti, the contact between the senses and
the sense-objects gives rise to cold and heat, pleasure
and pain.
These experiences are fleeting, they come and go.
Endure them bravely, O Arjuna. Only a person who
remains balanced in pleasure and pain and who is not
disturbed by these is fit for immortality (liberation)."
(Bhagvad Gita, 2.14, 2.15)

Chapter 13: Worship Your Work

"Pray as though everything depended on God.
Work as though everything depended on you."
Saint Augustine

The Bhagavad Gita declares that every action, when done with dedication, becomes sacred. Work is not separate from spirituality. It is an expression of it.

Approach your tasks, big or small, as acts of devotion. This mindset transforms the mundane into something deeply fulfilling.

Practice: Before starting a task, pause and mentally dedicate it to a higher purpose. Infuse it with your best effort and sincerity.

The question that how work can be spiritual when it involves worldly tasks, is answered beautifully by Lord Krishna in The Bhagvad Gita.

"Work must be done as a sacred offering, without attachment to results. When actions are performed in a spirit of worship, they purify the soul."
(Bhagvad Gita 3.9)

Chapter 14: Be Fearless

"The only thing we have to fear is fear itself." – Franklin D. Roosevelt

The Bhagavad Gita urges us to face life with courage, reminding us that fear binds us to illusions. Your soul is eternal, beyond harm or loss.

Fear restricts possibilities and clouds judgment. Recognizing your inner divinity helps you act boldly and embrace challenges with confidence.

Practice: When fear arises, repeat the affirmation, "I am fearless because I am eternal."

During Arjuna's breakdown on the battlefield, he
seeks courage from Lord Krishna,
"My limbs give way, my mouth is dry, my body
tremble I see evil omens, O Krishna. I cannot stand
here any longer. I will not fight."
(Bhagvad Gita, 1.28–30)

Lord Krishna lists fearlessness as the first diivine trait.
"Abhayam sattva-samshuddhir jnana-yoga-
vyavasthiti"
"Fearlessness, purity of heart, steadfastness in
knowledge and yoga are qualities of one born to a
divine nature."
(Bhagvad Gita, 16.1)

Chapter 15: Attachment- The Root of Misery

"The root of suffering is attachment."
Buddha

The Bhagavad Gita teaches that clinging to people, possessions, or outcomes leads to sorrow. Detachment brings freedom and contentment.

Loving without attachment means appreciating without ownership. This creates space for genuine relationships and inner peace.Detachment gives us inner freedom to act wisely.

Practice: Reflect on one thing you're overly attached to. Ask, "Can I let this go and still be happy?" Start practicing gentle detachment.

Arjuna is deeply disturbed as attachment to his kin
parayzes him with fear and sorrow. He says,
"O Krishna, seeing my own kinsmen gathered here,
eager to fight, my limbs fail and and my hair stands
on end."
(Bhagvad Gita, 1.28-1.30)

Lord Krishna, understanding his dilemma, explains,
"When a person dwells on objects of the senses,
attachment arises. Attachment clouds the mind,
leading to the destruction of self"
(Bhagvad Gita,2.62, 2.63)

Chapter 16: Meditation

"Meditation brings wisdom; lack of meditation leaves ignorance."
Dalai Lama

The Bhagavad Gita highlights meditation as a powerful tool to calm the restless mind. A peaceful mind enhances clarity, creativity, and joy.

Meditation isn't about stopping thoughts but observing them without attachment. This practice strengthens your inner stability and focus.

Practice: Spend five minutes daily in meditation. Focus on your breath and gently redirect your mind when it wavers.

Lord Krishna explains to Arjuna that discipline and constant self-connection can bring the mind under control.

"yuñjann evaṁ sadātmānaṁ yogī niyata-mānasaḥ
śāntiṁ nirvāṇa-paramāṁ mat-saṁsthām
adhigacchati"
(Bhagvad Gita, 6.15)

"Thus, constantly disciplining the mind, the yogi who is devoted to meditation, attains peace and liberation which is the supreme bliss that comes from union with Me."
(Bhagvad Gita, 6.15)

Chapter 17: All paths Lead to the Divine

"Truth is one; the wise call it by many names."
Rig Veda

The Bhagavad Gita teaches that every sincere path, whether devotion, wisdom, or action, leads to the ultimate truth. Follow the one that resonates with your heart.

Respecting diverse spiritual paths fosters unity and understanding. The goal is the same: connection with the divine within and beyond.

Practice: Explore different spiritual practices and see which nourishes your soul the most.

In The Bhagvad Gita, Lord Krishna assures Arjuna that whatever spiritual path a man follows with sincerity, it leads him to the divine. He further explains that only genuine intent and purity of heart are the things that are honoured by the divine.

"In whatever way people surrender unto Me, I reciprocate with them accordingly. O Arjuna, all paths walked in truth and devotion lead to me."
(Bhagavad Gita 4.11)

Author's interpretation:

No matter the name, the chant, the flame,
Each heart that seeks me is lit the same.
Through form or formless, word or deed,
The soul that loves shall surely reach me.

Paths may differ and steps may stray,
But all who walk in truth find the way.
For every prayer and act that's true
I receive them all, and walk with you.

Chapter 18: Inner Peace is True Wealth

"It is not the man who has too little, but the man who craves more, that is poor."
Seneca

The Bhagavad Gita reminds us that real wealth isn't in material possessions but in contentment and tranquility. Inner peace is priceless.

Chasing external riches often leads to emptiness. Cultivating gratitude and simplicity fills your life with lasting joy.

Practice: Begin a gratitude journal. List three things daily that bring you peace and happiness.

As Arjuna is evolving with Lord Krishna's teachings, he
finds it difficult to understand where true peace lies,
around us, or inside.

He asks Lord Krishna,
"Krishna, what brings real happiness in life? Is it found in
achievements and possessions, or in something deeper?"
(Bhagvad Gita, 2.7)

Lord Krishna, moved by Arjuna's curiosity for a deeper
understanding about human nature, responds,
"Just as the ocean remains full and undisturbed though
rivers flow into it from all sides, so too is the person who
remains unmoved by desire. That person finds peace, not
the one who chases desires."
(Bhagvad Gita, 2.70)

True wealth, Lord Krishna says, is a mind that is calm,
steady, and undisturbed.

Chapter 19: Be the Example

"Be the change that you wish to see in the world."
Mahatma Gandhi.

The Bhagavad Gita emphasizes leading through actions, not words. Living your values inspires others more than any speech.

People are drawn to authenticity. When you embody the qualities you advocate, you naturally uplift and influence those around you.

Practice: Identify one value you cherish. Today, let your actions reflect that value in everything you do.

Arjuna is unsure whether renouncing action or engaging in it is better.

He asks Lord Krishna,
"Krishna, if one is spiritually fulfilled, why act at all?"
(Bhagvad Gita, 3.22)

Lord Krishna answers,
"Great people must act, for others follow their example. I too act. It is not for gain, but to guide the world."
(Bhagvad Gita 3.21–22)

True leaders inspire through action. Even the enlightened must act selflessly to uplift others and set the right example.

Chapter 20: Marriage: A Union of Duty and Devotion

"It is better to live your own destiny imperfectly than to live an imitation of somebody else's life with perfection." (Bhagavad Gita, Chapter 3, Verse 35)

Marriage is a sacred partnership rooted in duty and devotion, where both individuals contribute to each other's spiritual growth. The Gita teaches that embracing one's unique roles and responsibilities with sincerity, rather than comparing to others, fosters harmony.

King Yudhishthira and Queen Draupadi from the Mahabharata embody this principle. Their unwavering commitment and mutual support during trials highlight how trust and shared purpose strengthen a marriage, aligning it with dharma and spiritual growth.

Chapter 21: Align With Your Inner Nature

"Nature does not hurry, yet everything is accomplished." – Lao Tzu

The Bhagavad Gita reminds us to act in harmony with our intrinsic nature. Trying to be something we're not leads to struggle, while alignment brings flow and fulfillment.

Your unique talents and qualities are gifts meant to be expressed authentically. When you honor them, life unfolds with ease and purpose.

Practice: Reflect on what activities feel natural and fulfilling to you. Spend time nurturing one of these today, without comparison or doubt.

Arjuna is internally conflicted fighting his own kin.
He argues that it is better to live by begging than
killing your own elders. He tells Lord Krishna,
"How can I fight against those I love? Isn't it better to
give up everything and live in peace?"
(Bhagvad Gita, 2.5)

Krishna chastises Arjuna's weekness and reminds him
that fighting this war is his kshatriya dharma. He
calmly tells Arjuna,
"Arjuna, you are a warrior by nature. This is your
path, your swadharma. To abandon your duty in fear
or attachment is not righteousness, it is weakness."
(Bhagvad Gita, 2.31)

Chapter 22: Knowledge Without Action is Futile

"An ounce of practice is worth more than tons of preaching."
Mahatma Gandhi

The Bhagavad Gita teaches that wisdom must translate into action. Knowledge alone is inert without deeds that reflect it.

True learning is seen in how you live your life. Apply what you know to transform yourself and positively influence others.

Practice: Choose one piece of wisdom you believe in but haven't acted upon. Take one concrete step to embody it today.

Chapter 23: Humility

"It is very often nothing but our own vanity that deceives us."
Jane Austen, Pride and Prejudice

The Bhagavad Gita urges humility, reminding us that true greatness comes from serving without arrogance. Pride limits growth, while humility expands possibilities.

When you let go of the need for recognition, your work gains depth and authenticity. Ego-free action uplifts you and those around you.

Practice: The next time you accomplish something, quietly acknowledge your success without seeking praise. Let your actions speak for themselves.

Chapter 24: Everythimg is Interconnected

"When we try to pick out anything by itself, we find it hitched to everything else in the universe."
John Muir

The Bhagavad Gita teaches that all beings are part of the same divine essence. Recognizing this unity fosters compassion and harmony.

Understanding interconnection dissolves barriers of division. It encourages kindness and cooperation, knowing that we're all threads in the same fabric.

Practice: Perform one act of kindness today for someone outside your immediate circle, acknowledging the oneness of all life.

Still overwhelmed, Arjuna lowers his how and asks
Lord Krishna,
"Krishna, in this vast chaos, do we truly belong to
one another? Or are we all just alone in our paths?"
(Bhagvad Gita, 6.30-6.31)

Lord Krishna calmly replies,
"No one is separate, Arjuna. I dwell in all beings, and
all beings dwell in Me."
(Bhagavad Gita, 6.30)

Chapter 25: Be selfless in Service

"The best way to find yourself is to lose yourself in the service of others."
Mahatma Gandhi

The Bhagavad Gita emphasises selfless service (seva) as a path to joy and enlightenment. Serving others without expecting rewards purifies the heart.

True service arises from empathy and love, not obligation. It enriches your soul and brings profound contentment.

Acts of service create a ripple effect of kindness and gratitude. They nurture both the giver and the receiver.

Practice: Offer help today where it's needed most, whether it's a kind word, a thoughtful gesture, or simply your time.

Chapter 26: Manifestation- Aligning Thoughts with Purpose

"When you want something, all the universe conspires in helping you to achieve it."
Paulo Coleho, The Alchemist

The Bhagavad Gita teaches that our thoughts and intentions shape our reality. By focusing the mind on what we wish to achieve and aligning it with our higher purpose, we attract those outcomes into our lives.

Manifestation begins with clarity of intention and unwavering faith, as what we consistently think about becomes a part of our being.

By practicing mindful thoughts, purposeful actions, and unwavering faith, manifestation becomes a natural extension of one's spiritual journey, as emphasized in The Bhagvad Gita

Lord Krishna hints at the power of conscious manifestation in The Bhagvad Gita-

"When one aligns their thoughts, desires and actions with devotion, purity and purpose, the divine supports their journey. Manifestation becomes grace in action. It is not forced, but flowing through surrender and alignment."
(Bhagvad Gita, 15.15)

"I am seated in everyone's heart, and from me come memory, knowledge, and reason."
(Bhagavad Gita 15.15)

Chapter 27: Peace Through Detachment

"Some of us think holding on makes us strong, but sometimes it is letting go."
Hermann Hesse

The Bhagavad Gita emphasizes releasing attachment to outcomes, possessions and even relationships. Letting go frees you to live fully.

Releasing attachments doesn't mean indifference; it means trusting the flow of life. It opens doors to new opportunities.

Practice: Identify one thing you've been holding onto tightly. Today, take a step to release it, whether it's a grudge, fear, or expectation.

Lord Krishna teaches that inner peace is not found by escaping the world, but by acting in it with detachment.

"When one gives up all desires born of the mind and is satisfied in the Self alone, that person is truly at peace."
(Bhagavad Gita 2.55)

"The person who abandons all desires and moves through life without longing, without the sense of 'I' or 'mine,' attains peace."
(Bhagvad Gita 2.71)

Lord Krishna lovingly reveals that clinging to desires is the source of inner unrest. He emphasises that attachment is the root of inner turmoil. Detachment, not indifference but calm acceptance, is the doorway to peace.

Chapter 28: Perseverance Defines You

"It does not matter how slowly you go as long as you do not stop."
Confucius

The Bhagavad Gita celebrates resilience and unwavering effort. Success isn't about speed but about staying committed to your journey.

Every step forward, no matter how small, builds strength and character. Your persistence shapes your destiny.

Practice: Break a big goal into smaller steps. Focus on completing one step today, celebrating your progress along the way.

Chapter 29: Empathy- The Path to Inner Peace

Lord Krishna says:
"He who, through the likeness of the self, sees all living beings as one and the same, both in their happiness and distress, is considered a perfect yogi."
(Bhagvad Gita, 6.32)

This verse highlights the importance of empathy by urging individuals to view others' joys and sorrows as their own.

The Bhagavad Gita emphasizes empathy as a crucial aspect of human behavior, highlighting the need to understand and share the feelings of others.

It teaches that empathy is essential for harmony and inner peace. It calls for understanding the feelings and perspectives of others, transcending selfish desires, and acting with compassion.

By practicing empathy, we align with the teachings of the Bhagavad Gita and cultivate a peaceful life rooted in kindness, compassion, and unity.

From a psychological stand point, living with empathy involves developing emotional intelligence, self-awareness, and active listening skills. Empathy allows us to connect deeply with others, fostering healthier relationships and greater personal well-being.

Living with empathy is a skill that can be cultivated through intentional practices, ultimately leading to more meaningful connections and a balanced, peaceful life.

Practice: Put yourself in another person's shoes to see the world from their viewpoint. Speak kindly, please veb during disagreements.

Chapter 30: Overcoming Despair

"Ashochyaan anva-shochas tvam prajna-vadaamsh cha bhaashase; Gatasoon agatasoon cha naanushochanti panditaah."
(Bhagavad Gita, Chapter 2, Verse 11)

"You are mourning for that which is not worthy of grief. The wise lament neither for the living nor the dead."

The Bhagavad Gita teaches that despair arises from attachment and ignorance of our true nature. The eternal soul remains unaffected by worldly sorrows. Grief, though natural, stems from identifying with temporary aspects of life, such as the body, possessions, or relationships. By focusing on the eternal, one can transcend sorrow.

When Arjuna was overwhelmed with despair on the
battlefield, Krishna reminded him of his higher purpose
and the eternal nature of the soul.

The Gita teaches that during times of depression, we must:
1. Recognize that suffering is temporary.
2. Focus on performing our duties without attachment to
outcomes.
3. Seek spiritual knowledge and faith in the divine plan.

By cultivating inner strength, self-awareness, and
detachment, we can rise above moments of deep sorrow
and reconnect with our true self.

Chapter 31: Adapt to Change Gracefully

"It is not the strongest of the species that survive, nor the most intelligent, but the one most responsive to change."
Charles Darwin

The Bhagavad Gita teaches that change is inevitable and resistance leads to suffering. Embracing change allows us to grow and align with the flow of life's rythm.

Lord Krishna reminds Arjuna,
"The only thing that is constant is change. Growth happens when we accept change without fear)
(Bhagvad Gita, 2.47)

Adapting to change is not about giving up but about finding strength in flexibility. It's through change that we discover new dimensions of ourselves.

Practice: The next time a change disrupts your routine, pause and ask, "What can I learn from this?" Focus on opportunities, not obstacles.

Chapter 32: Contentment is Power

"He who is contented is rich."
Lao Tzu

The Bhagavad Gita emphasizes that contentment is the greatest wealth. Craving for more only breeds dissatisfaction, while gratitude brings lasting joy.

When you appreciate what you have, you break free from the cycle of endless desires. Gratitude enhances your well-being.

Practice: Take a moment to appreciate three simple things in your life, a warm meal, a kind word, or the air you breathe.

Chapter 33: Embrace Self- Discipline

"Discipline is the bridge between goals and
accomplishment."
Jim Rohn

The **Bhagavad Gita** highlights self-discipline as the
foundation of personal growth. Without discipline,
potential remains unrealized.

When Arjuna expresses concern over the restless nature
of the mind, he responds by emphasizing self-discipline
(ātma-saṁyama) as the foundation of spiritual progress
and inner peace.
(Bhagvad Gita, 6.5)

Self-discipline isn't about restriction but about directing
your energy toward meaningful pursuits. It helps you stay
focused and resilient.

Practice: Set a small, achievable goal for the week. Stick
to it consistently, even when it feels inconvenient.
Celebrate your effort.

Chapter 34: Wisdom Lies in Simplicity

"Simplicity is the ultimate sophistication."
Leonardo Da Vinci

The Bhagavad Gita teaches that simplicity leads to harmony. A cluttered life, physically or mentally, creates unrest while simplicity fosters peace.

By embracing simplicity, you free yourself from distractions and focus on what truly matters. It makes life more meaningful.

Simplicity doesn't mean lack. It means focusing on what truly matters. A life rooted in simplicity is rich in meaning.

Practice: Simplify one area of your life today declutter a space, clear your schedule, or let go of an unnecessary thought.

"amānitvam adambhitvam ahiṁsā kṣāntir ārjavam
ācāryopāsanaṁ śaucaṁ sthairyam ātma-vinigrahaḥ"
(Bhagvad Gita,13.8)

Ārjavam here means simplicity. Lord Krishna describes
simplicity as a mind and life free from mental clutter
caused by duplicity, pride, and inner conflict.

He emphasis that cultivating simplicity is not optional,
but essential for spiritual evolution.

Chapter 35: Align Actions with Values

"Happiness is when what you think, what you say, and what you do are in harmony."
Mahatma Gandhi

The Bhagavad Gita stresses the importance of integrity. Actions aligned with values bring inner peace and self-respect.

Living authentically builds trust, both with yourself and others. When your actions mirror your values, you experience true fulfillment.

Practice: Identify one value you hold dear. Make a conscious effort to act on it in all your interactions.

Chapter 36: Cultivate Patience

"Patience is bitter, but its fruit is sweet."
Jean-Jacques Rousseau

The Bhagavad Gita teaches that patience is essential for growth. Hurrying through life often leads to mistakes and missed lessons.

Patience allows you to navigate challenges with grace and await the right opportunities. It's a silent strength that transforms outcomes.

Practice: When you feel rushed, pause and take five deep breaths. Remind yourself, "Good things take time."

Chapter 37: Let Go of Judgement

"When you judge another, you do not define them; you define yourself."
Wayne Dyer

The Bhagavad Gita advises against judging others, as everyone is on their unique journey. Compassion fosters connection, while judgment creates division.

Judging others often reflects inner insecurities. Letting go of judgment allows you to see others with empathy and understanding.

Practice: The next time you catch yourself judging someone, pause and think of one positive trait they possess. Shift your perspective.

Chapter 38: Resilience in Adversity

"The oak fought the wind and was broken, the willow bent when it must and survived."
Robert Jordan

The Bhagavad Gita teaches that resilience is key to overcoming life's trials. Like a tree bending with the wind, flexibility ensures survival.

Challenges are opportunities in disguise. Resilience allows you to grow stronger and wiser through adversity.

Practice: When facing a setback, write down three things you've learned from it. Use these lessons to guide your next steps.

Chapter 39: Follow the Middle Path

"Virtue is the golden mean between two extremes."
Aristotle

The Bhagavad Gita emphasizes moderation in all aspects of life. Extremes often lead to imbalance and suffering.

The middle path nurtures harmony and prevents burnout. It allows you to enjoy life's pleasures without being enslaved by them.

Practice: Reflect on areas where you tend toward excess or deprivation. Aim for a balanced approach in one of these areas today.

Chapter 40: Be Like a Baby

"In the beginner's mind there are many possibilities; in the expert's mind there are few."
Shunryu Suzuki

The Bhagavad Gita reminds us to stay open to learning. A rigid mind blocks growth, while curiosity keeps the spirit alive.

Approaching life with humility and curiosity ensures continuous growth and deeper understanding.

Practice: Approach a familiar task as if doing it for the first time. Observe new insights or feelings that arise.

Chapter 41: The Art of Self- Control

"He who conquers himself is the mightiest warrior."
Confucius

The Bhagavad Gita emphasizes that mastering the self is the greatest victory. Self-control is the foundation of a peaceful and disciplined life.

When you control your emotions and impulses, you act with clarity and wisdom. This mastery brings harmony within and with the world around you.

Practice: The next time you feel an impulse, whether it's anger or indulgence, pause, take a deep breath and choose a response that aligns with your higher self.

Chapter 42: Focus to Make Goals Real

"You become what you think about."
Earl Nightingale

The Bhagavad Gita teaches that where your attention goes, energy flows. A focused mind achieves greatness, while a scattered one achieves little.

Your thoughts shape your actions and destiny. By focusing on positive and purposeful thoughts, you align your life with your aspirations.

Practice: Dedicate 10 minutes today to a task without any distractions. Observe how much more effective and fulfilling your effort becomes.

Chapter 42: Accept What You Cannot Change

"God, grant me the serenity to accept the things I cannot change."
Reinhold Niebuhr

The Bhagavad Gita advises surrendering to life's inevitable realities. Acceptance doesn't mean giving up; it means finding peace within challenges.

Resistance drains energy, while acceptance restores it. By embracing what is, you gain the clarity to act on what can be changed.

Practice: Identify one situation you've been resisting. Write down what you can and cannot control about it. Let go of the rest.

Chapter 44: Your Body, The Sacred Temple

"Shariram yad avāpnoti yac chāpy utkramati īśvarah;
gṛhītvaitāni samyāti vāyur gandhān ivāśayat."
(Bhagavad Gita, Chapter 15, Verse 8)

"When the soul takes on a body or leaves it, it carries the mind and senses, just as the wind carries fragrances from their source."

The Bhagavad Gita teaches that the body should be treated as a temple, cared for with discipline, nourishment, and mindfulness. It is not to be worshipped or overly indulged, but rather respected as an instrument for spiritual evolution. Maintaining the body through healthy habits, exercise, and moderation allows us to live harmoniously and fulfill our dharma..

The body is a sacred vessel for the soul, enabling it to experience the world and fulfill its purpose. While the soul is eternal, the body is its temporary abode, requiring care and respect to perform its duties. Neglecting or abusing the body disrupts the balance necessary for spiritual growth, while respecting it aligns us with the divine purpose.

Practice: By honoring the body as a divine gift, we cultivate balance and gratitude, allowing the soul to shine through its physical form.

Chapter 45: The Sound of Silence

"Silence is a source of great strength."
Lao Tzu

The Bhagavad Gita teaches that inner silence reveals truth and wisdom. Amid noise, silence is where clarity resides.

In stillness, you connect with your higher self. This connection guides you toward right action and peace. Silence helps you listen better, reflect deeply, and respond thoughtfully. It is a tool for emotional and mental balance.

The sound of silence is the most beautiful noise.

Practice: Spend five minutes in silence everyday, focusing only on your breath. Let this stillness center and rejuvenate you.

Chapter 46: Divine Potential- Embrace All Abilities

"The wise see with equal vision a learned and gentle priest, a cow, an elephant, a dog, and even an outcast"
The Bhagvad Gita

The Bhagavad Gita emphasizes that the true essence of a person lies in their soul, not in their physical or external attributes. All beings are equal in the eyes of the Divine, regardless of their abilities or circumstances.

People with disabilities are as much a part of the divine creation as anyone else. Their worth is not defined by physical or mental limitations but by the eternal soul within.

The Bhagvad Gita teaches us to look beyond appearances and embrace everyone with respect, compassion, and understanding, fostering inclusivity and equality.

Chapter 47: Embrace Impermanence

Arjuna asked Lord Krishna on the battlefield of Mahabharata "Tell me something that will make someone going through hard times happy and someone who has everything sad". Lord Krishna replied "This too shall pass"

The Bhagavad Gita teaches that all things, good and bad, are temporary. Embracing impermanence helps you live fully in the moment.

When you accept that nothing lasts forever, you cherish life's fleeting beauty and release unnecessary attachments.

Practice: When you experience joy or challenges, remind yourself, "This too shall pass." Let this awareness ground you.

Chapter 48: Act With Courage, Not Fear

"Courage is resistance to fear, mastery of fear, not absence of fear."
Mark Twain

The Bhagavad Gita encourages bravery in the face of uncertainty. Fear paralyzes, but courage moves you forward.

Courage isn't about being fearless; it's about acting despite fear. Each step builds confidence and strength.

Practice: Take one small action today toward a goal that intimidates you. Celebrate the courage it took to move forward.

Chapter 49: Find Joy in Little Things

"Enjoy the little things, for one day you may look back
and realize they were the big things."
Robert Brault

The Bhagavad Gita reminds us that happiness isn't found
in grand achievements but in appreciating life's simple
moments.

By finding joy in the ordinary, you cultivate a life of
gratitude and fulfillment. Small joys are the foundation
of a meaningful life.

Practice: Notice one small thing that brings you joy
today, a smile, a breeze, or a quiet moment. Savor it fully.

Chapter 50: Envy and Jealousy- Our Worst Enemies

There is neither intelligence nor stability of mind for the envious person, and without peace, how can there be happiness?"
(Bhagavad Gita, Chapter 2, Verse 66)

The Bhagavad Gita teaches that jealousy and envy arise from attachment, ignorance, and a lack of self-awareness. These emotions create disharmony within, clouding our ability to see others' successes as part of the collective good.

By overcoming jealousy, we free ourselves from negative energy and foster a sense of inner peace and contentment.

Jealousy and envy are deeply disruptive emotions that erode our peace and happiness. They stem from constant comparisons and a sense of lack, creating a mental state that is far removed from contentment.

Jealousy and envy create a sense of inner turmoil that robs us of our ability to enjoy life. It prevents us from celebrating others' successes and blinds us to our potential, replacing positivity with frustration and inadequacy.

The Gita teaches that jealousy is rooted in attachment and ignorance. As Lord Krishna says, "An envious mind cannot attain peace or happiness." Only by recognizing the futility of envy and embracing self-awareness can we liberate ourselves from its grip.

When jealousy dominates, the outcomes are invariably harmful. Anger and resentment grow, damaging our mental health. Relationships suffer as trust and compassion give way to bitterness. We feel disconnected from our true self, leading to unhappiness and emotional fatigue.

By letting go of jealousy, we free ourselves from its toxic effects, paving the way for clarity, inner harmony, and lasting joy.

Practice: Replace envious thoughts with admiration and inspiration from others' success.
Set personal goals and celebrate your progress without comparing yourself to others.
Repeat affirmations like, "I am enough," or "I celebrate the success of others as I walk my unique path."

Chapter 51: Learn From Failure

"Success is not final, failure is not fatal: It is the courage to continue that counts."
Winston Churchill

The Bhagavad Gita teaches that failure is a stepping stone, not a dead end. Each setback carries lessons essential for growth.

Failures build resilience and teach humility. By viewing them as opportunities, you transform obstacles into pathways for success.

Practice: Reflect on a recent failure. Identify one lesson it taught you and how you can apply it moving forward.

Chapter 52: The Power of Humility

"It is always the secure who are humble."
G.K. Chesterton

The Bhagavad Gita highlights humility as a cornerstone of wisdom. True strength comes from knowing you are a part of something greater.

Humility opens doors to learning and connection. It allows you to value others and grow beyond ego.

Practice: In your next conversation, focus on listening more than speaking. Appreciate the perspectives of others without judgment.

Chapter 53: Choose Your Company Wisely

"You are the average of the five people you spend the most time with."
Jim Rohn

The Bhagavad Gita advises associating with those who uplift and inspire. Your environment shapes your thoughts and actions.

Positive company motivates you to grow, while negative influences pull you down. Surround yourself with people who align with your values.

Practice: Evaluate your close relationships. Spend more time with those who encourage your growth and less with those who drain your energy.

Chapter 54: Be Anchored in Values, Not Outcomes

"Try not to become a person of success, but rather a person of value."
Albert Einstein

The Bhagavad Gita teaches that lasting fulfillment comes from living a life rooted in values, not chasing fleeting achievements.

When you prioritize values, success follows naturally. It ensures your journey is meaningful, regardless of the outcome.

Practice: Identify one core value you hold dear, like honesty or kindness. Make a conscious effort to embody it today.

Chapter 55: Accept Imperfection

"There is a crack in everything, that's how the light gets in."
Leonard Cohen

The Bhagavad Gita reminds us that perfection is an illusion. Embracing flaws,yours and others',brings peace and understanding.

Perfectionism creates stress, while acceptance fosters growth. Imperfections are opportunities for compassion and learning.

Practice: The next time you notice a flaw in yourself or someone else, reframe it as a unique characteristic or potential strength.

Chapter 56: Compassion- The Bridge to Divine Love

"One who is free from malice towards all beings, friendly and compassionate, free from attachment and ego, and balanced in pleasure and pain, is dear to Me."
The Bhagvad Gita

The Bhagavad Gita says that true compassion comes from seeing everyone as connected, like parts of one big family. When we are kind and caring, we rise above selfishness and anger, and our hearts grow lighter and happier. Compassion isn't just about feeling sorry for others, it is about choosing to care, forgive, and help whenever we can.

Lord Krishna reminds us that by being compassionate, we don't just help others; we also grow closer to God and find peace within ourselves.

Chapter 57:Detach From Praise and Criticism

"Don't let compliments go to your head and don't let criticism go to your heart."
Lysa TerKeurst

The Bhagavad Gita advises staying balanced amidst praise and blame. Both are fleeting and should not define your self-worth.

Anchoring yourself in inner validation frees you from the highs and lows of external opinions. You remain focused on your truth.

Practice: When receiving praise or criticism today, take a moment to reflect. Thank the person, but let your self-worth remain independent of their words.

Chapter 58: Live With Intention

"An unexamined life is not worth living."
Socrates

The Bhagavad Gita encourages deliberate living. Acting with awareness transforms even mundane tasks into meaningful experiences.

When you live with intention, every action aligns with your greater purpose. It brings clarity and fulfillment to your days.

Practice: Before starting your day, set one clear intention, whether it's to practice patience, kindness, or focus. Let it guide your actions.

Chapter 59: Self Preservation- The Foundation of Inner Strength

"To be yourself in a world that is constantly trying to make you something else is the greatest accomplishment."
Ralph Waldo Emerson

The Gita emphasizes that self-preservation is not selfishness but self-awareness. Krishna advises Arjuna to prioritize the well-being of the self by aligning with dharma (duty) and maintaining physical, mental, and spiritual health.

The self is the cornerstone of existence. By protecting and nurturing the body and mind, one becomes capable of fulfilling responsibilities and pursuing higher spiritual goals.

Without self-preservation, individuals become vulnerable to burnout, stress, and disconnection from their purpose. Taking care of oneself is essential for serving others and achieving lasting peace.

According to psychologists, self-care is crucial for mental health. Practices like setting boundaries, seeking support, and balancing work and rest are proven to enhance resilience and productivity.

Practice: Dedicate time for mindfulness and meditation, engage in activities that nourish your body, such as exercise and healthy eating. Learn to say no to unnecessary demands.

Arjuna, overwhelmed and fatigued, asks Lord Krishna,
"Krishna, sometimes I feel overwhelmed. My mind gets
tired, my body feels heavy. Is it wrong to step back or
take a break from discipline?"

Smiling gently, Lord Krishna replies,
"Arjuna, true discipline does not mean denying yourself
rest."

Arjuna:
"So, you mean I don't have to force myself all the time?"

Lord Krishna:
"Yes, everything in moderation is what will give you
peace."

Arjuna:
"So rest is not laziness, but wisdom?"

Lord Krishna:
"Exactly. To pause, to recharge, to care for your body
and mind is not weakness, but strength.
It is through balance that you become steady like a flame
untouched by the wind."

(Bhagvad Gita 6.16, 6.17)

Chapter 60: See Divinity Everywhere

"Everything is connected, we are all one."
Nikola Tesla

The Bhagavad Gita reveals the divine presence in all beings and creations. Recognizing this unity fosters respect, love, and harmony.

When you see divinity in everything, life becomes sacred. Every interaction and experience takes on deeper meaning.

Practice: Spend a moment today observing nature or interacting with someone, and remind yourself, "This too is divine."

Chapter 61: Practice Gratitude Everyday

"Gratitude is not only the greatest of virtues, but the parent of all others."
Cicero

The Bhagavad Gita teaches that contentment comes from acknowledging the blessings in your life. Gratitude shifts focus from lack to abundance.

When you cultivate gratitude, even challenges seem smaller, and life becomes more fulfilling. It creates a positive mindset that attracts peace.

Practice: Each night, write down three things you're grateful for. Reflect on how they made your day better.

Chapter 62: Live Beyond The Ego

"Man is not what he thinks he is, he is what he hides."
Andrè Malraux

The Bhagavad Gita urges shedding the ego, which clouds judgment and fosters selfishness. True strength lies in humility and selflessness.

Living beyond ego allows you to connect deeply with others and align with higher wisdom. It fosters genuine relationships and clarity.

Practice: When faced with a decision today, ask yourself, "Am I choosing this out of pride or for the greater good?"

Chapter 63: Speech and Karma

"The desire to know what is going on in the lives of others often leads to gossip, which corrupts both speaker and listener alike."
Anomymus

The Bhagavad Gita emphasizes self-discipline, truthfulness, and purity of speech. Gossiping is seen as a misuse of speech, which creates negativity and distances us from higher spiritual values.

Gossip leads negative karma by spreading negativity, impacting both the speaker and listener by fostering division and ignorance.

Practice: Before talking about another person, think about the psychological impact them and imagine how you would feel if someone said the same about you.

Chapter 64: The Power of Forgiveness

"The weak can never forgive. Forgiveness is the attribute of the strong."
Mahatma Gandhi

The Bhagavad Gita emphasizes forgiveness as a path to freedom. Holding onto grudges only burdens the soul.

Forgiving doesn't condone wrongs; it liberates you from anger and resentment. It allows you to move forward with peace.

"When you can forgive, you are free. You free yourself from the negativity that holds you back from living a truly magical life."
Rhonda Byrne, The Magic

Forgiveness is an act of self-liberation. Holding onto resentment traps you in negativity and blocks the flow of positive energy and abundance into your life. By forgiving, you release emotional burdens and open yourself to gratitude, happiness, and fulfillment.

Practice: Recall someone who wronged you. Instead of holding resentment, silently wish them peace and let go of the hurt.

Chapter 65: Be the Change you Seek

"Be the change that you wish to see in the world."
Mahatma Gandhi

The Bhagavad Gita teaches that transformation begins within. Instead of waiting for others to change, embody the qualities you desire.

When you live as an example, you inspire others. Your actions create a ripple effect of positive change.

Practice: Identify one quality, like patience or honesty you wish to see in others. Practice it yourself in every interaction today.

Chapter 66: Happiness Lies Within

"Happiness is a state of mind. Focus on joy and gratitude to attract more of it into your life."

The Bhagavad Gita teaches that true happiness comes from within and is achieved through self-control, detachment, and inner peace.

It advises letting go of desires and expectations, staying balanced in success and failure, and focusing on selfless action.

Practice: Train yourself to accept both positive and negative experiences with composure, recognizing that all are temporary.

Chapter 67: Overcome Fear Through Faith

"Fear is only as deep as the mind allows."
Japanese Proverb

The Bhagavad Gita teaches that faith dissolves fear. When you trust in a higher power, fear loses its grip on your mind.

Faith creates courage and opens pathways to solutions that fear obscures. It empowers you to act despite uncertainties.

Practice: When fear arises, repeat a mantra or affirmation that resonates with you, like "I am guided and protected."

Chapter 68: Greed- The Endless Chase

"Earth provides enough to satisfy every man's needs, but not every man's greed."
Mahatma Gandhi

In The Bhagvad Gita, Krishna condemns greed as a destructive force that arises from uncontrolled desires. Greed blinds the mind, disrupts inner peace, and leads to unethical actions.

Greed is a form of spiritual ignorance. It arises from identifying oneself with material possessions instead of recognizing the eternal self.

Greed leads to exploitation, dissatisfaction, and inner turmoil. By overcoming it, one cultivates generosity, simplicity, and contentment.

In psychology, greed is linked to fear of scarcity and insecurity. Overcoming greed involves shifting from a mindset of lack to one of abundance and gratitude.

Practice: Reflect on needs versus wants before making decisions, share resources with those in need, Meditate on the impermanence of material wealth.

Lord Krishna identifies desire and greed (kāma and lobha) as the enemies of human will.

Arjuna asks Lord Krishna,
"How does greed affect one's wisdom, O Krishna?
(Bhagvad Gita 3.38–3.40)

Lord Krishna replies,
"As fire is covered by smoke, a mirror by dust, and a fetus by the womb, so is wisdom obscured by greed. It exists in our senses, our mind and our intellect. Greed deludes the embodied soul by clouding its knowledge."
(Bhagavad Gita 3.38–3.40)

Chapter 69: Detach But Love Deeply

"Asaktaḥ sarva-karmāṇi sannyasyādhyātma-cetasā"
The Bhagvad Gita

The Bhagvad Gita inspires us to perform all actions without attachment, surrendering to a higher consciousness.

True love and relationships are about giving without the constant expectation of return. Detachment isn't apathy, it is about letting go of control while still offering care and affection.

Practice: Love others selflessly, focus on their well-being, and let go of the fear of losing them. Balance your emotions with reason.

Chapter 70: Align With your Purpose

"The meaning of life is to find your gift. The purpose of life is to give it away."
Pablo Picasso

The Bhagavad Gita stresses the importance of living your dharma, your unique purpose. Life feels fulfilled when aligned with your true calling.

When you honor your purpose, you contribute to the greater good and experience inner joy.

Practice: Reflect on your passions and strengths. Take one small step today to align your actions with your purpose.

Chapter 71: Embrace Change as Growth

"Change is the law of life. and those who look only to the past or present are certain to miss the future."
John F. Kennedy

The Bhagavad Gita reminds us that life is ever-changing. Resisting change leads to suffering, while accepting it paves the way for growth.

Change allows you to adapt, evolve, and discover new strengths. It's a natural part of the journey to self-realization.

Practice: When faced with change today, identify one positive outcome it could bring. Focus on that instead of the discomfort.

Chapter 72: Lead with Compassion

"If you want others to be happy, practice compassion. If you want to be happy, practice compassion."
Dalai Lama

The Bhagavad Gita highlights compassion as a divine quality. Being kind and understanding strengthens bonds and brings inner peace.

Compassion enriches your relationships and uplifts those around you. It bridges differences and nurtures harmony.

Practice: Perform one random act of kindness today. Offer a smile, lend a helping hand, or speak words of encouragement.

Chapter 73: Kindness-Life's Greatest Virtue

"Be kind whenever possible. It is always possible."
Dalai Lama

This quote echoes The Bhagvad Gita's philosophy by reminding us that kindness is not dependent on circumstances; it is a choice we can make every day, regardless of the situation.

The Bhagavad Gita emphasizes the importance of kindness as an essential aspect of dharma (righteous living).

This teaching underlines that true spirituality lies in embracing kindness, not just as an act but as a way of life.

Kindness, in its purest form, is the selfless act of recognizing the divine essence within all beings and treating them with compassion, understanding, and love.

In essence, kindness is the universal language of the soul. Itreminder of our shared humanity and the divinity within each of us.

Practice: Reflect before speaking or acting. Ask yourself if your words or deeds are uplifting and kind.

Chapter 74: Redefine Success Beyond the Material

"Happiness consists not in having much, but in being content with little."
Marguerite Gardiner

The Bhagavad Gita reveals that true happiness comes from contentment, not external achievements. Contentment brings stability and joy.

Success isn't merely wealth or fame but attaining wisdom, self-awareness, and understanding life's truths. Trying to accumulate wealth whilst comparing to those around you causes anxiety.

Knowledge transforms our perception and enhances inner peace. Shifting focus to personal growth creates balance in our lives.

These teachings remind us to go beyond conventional thinking and see life from a higher perspective, blending practical wisdom with profound spirituality.

Practice: Let go of the constant need to "keep up" with societal expectations of wealth and status. Focus more on building meaningful relationships rather than building social status. Transcend the need to adhere to social norms and you will gradually feel anxiety releasing it's grip on you.

Chapter 75: Be a Lifelong Learner

"Education is the most powerful weapon which you can use to change the world."
Nelson Mandela

The Bhagavad Gita encourages continual learning. Wisdom isn't static; it's a journey of discovery and growth.

A curious and open mind keeps you grounded and adaptable. Learning enriches your perspective and sharpens your intellect.

Practice: Dedicate 15 minutes today to learning something new, read a book, listen to a podcast, or explore a new skill.

Chapter 76: Act Without Ego

"Ego is the enemy of truth."
Mahatma Gandhi

The Bhagavad Gita warns that ego blinds you to reality. By acting selflessly, you align with your true purpose and find greater peace.

Selfless actions bring fulfillment and connect you to the divine. Ego-driven choices often lead to conflict and dissatisfaction.

Practice: In your next task, focus on the impact it will have on others rather than seeking personal recognition.

Chapter 77: Foster Inner Resilience

"It is not the strongest of the species that survives, but the one most adaptable to change."
Charles Darwin

The Bhagavad Gita teaches that resilience comes from inner strength. Life's challenges are meant to refine, not break you.

Resilience enables you to face difficulties with courage and perseverance. It transforms adversity into opportunities.

Practice: Recall a past challenge you overcame. Reflect on the strength it revealed within you and apply that perspective to your current struggles.

Chapter 78: Overthinking- The Greatest Hurdle

"A day of worry is more exhausting than a week of work."
John Lubbock

The Bhagavad Gita advises against overthinking, which drains energy and clouds judgment. A calm mind leads to wise decisions.

Overthinking creates problems that don't exist. Simplicity and clarity are found in trusting your instincts and acting decisively.

Practice: The next time you catch yourself overthinking, pause and write down your thoughts. Evaluate which ones are truly worth your energy.

Chapter 79: Honour the Power of Detachment

"The root of suffering is attachment."
Buddha

The Bhagavad Gita explains that attachment to outcomes or possessions creates suffering. Detachment frees you to live authentically.

Detachment doesn't mean indifference but rather balance. It lets you enjoy life's gifts without clinging to them.

Practice: Identify one thing you're overly attached to. It can be a goal or a material possession. Practice letting go, even if only mentally.

Chapter 80: The Journey is The Destination

"It is good to have an end to journey toward; but it is the journey that matters, in the end."
Ursula K. Le Guin

The Bhagavad Gita reminds us that life is about the process, not just the results. Enjoying the journey enriches the destination.

When you focus on the present moment, life becomes more vibrant and rewarding. Each step holds its own joy and lesson.

Practice: As you work on a task today, focus on the process rather than the outcome. Savor the experience fully.

Chapter 81: The Danger of Showing off Material Wealth

"You are not your bank account, nor your possessions."
Ekhart Tolle, A new earth

The Gita warns against being attached to material possessions. Krishna teaches that wealth and status are temporary and should be used to serve a higher purpose rather than to fuel ego or pride.

True fulfillment comes from inner contentment, not external validation. Displaying wealth for admiration creates an illusion of happiness and fosters envy in others.

Excessive focus on materialism leads to emptiness and dissatisfaction. Genuine joy arises from humility, gratitude, and connection with others.

According to psychology the need to show off stems from insecurity and comparison. Studies show that intrinsic goals like personal growth and relationships bring greater happiness than extrinsic goals like wealth or fame.

Practice: Practice gratitude for what you have without seeking validation, engage in acts of generosity or charity, focus on building meaningful relationships over accumulating possessions.

Chapter 82: Rise Above Small Mindedness

"Great minds discuss ideas; average minds discuss events; small minds discuss people."
Eleanor Roosevelt

The Bhagavad Gita teaches to avoid petty thinking and gossip. A higher perspective focuses on meaningful ideas and purpose.

Rising above small-mindedness frees you from negativity and opens your mind to growth and creativity. It nurtures wisdom and clarity.

Practice: The next time a conversation drifts toward criticism or gossip, steer it toward constructive topics or positive ideas.

Chapter 83: Cultivate a Steady Mind

"An untroubled mind, no longer seeking to consider what is right and what is wrong, a mind beyond judgments, watches and understands."
Buddha

The Bhagavad Gita teaches that a steady mind is the foundation of inner peace. Emotional turbulence disturbs clarity, while steadiness fosters balance.

A calm and focused mind is less reactive and more deliberate, enabling wiser decisions and greater fulfillment.

Practice: Spend a few moments each day observing your thoughts without reacting to them. Let them pass like clouds in the sky.

Chapter 84: Nurture Inner Strength

"He who conquers himself is the mightiest warrior."
Confucius

The Bhagavad Gita reveals that true strength comes from mastering your inner world. Controlling your emotions, desires, and fears makes you invincible.

Inner strength enables you to face adversity with grace and persevere through challenges with resilience.

Practice: Identify one area where you feel weak, be it impatience, fear, or doubt and take a small step today to address and overcome it.

Chapter 85: Honouring Your Parents- A Divine Duty

"It is a sin to neglect or disrespect one's parents"
-Mahatma Gandhi

The Gita reminds us that parents are earthly manifestations of divine love and care. They nurture, guide, and sustain us, making their role sacred. Krishna teaches us to honor and serve them as an expression of our gratitude and dharma (duty).

The Gita views parents as God's representatives who provide us with life, love, and lessons.

Respecting them is not just a social duty but a spiritual practice that aligns us with dharma and brings harmony to family life.

Practice: Be great ful for their love and sacrifices.

Change 86: Embrace Courage Amid Uncertainty

"Courage is resistance to fear, mastery of fear. It is not absence of fear."
Mark Twain

The Bhagavad Gita teaches that courage lies in acting despite fear. Challenges test your faith and reveal your inner potential.

Lord Krishna says that as human beings, all we fear is uncertainty about outcomes and future events.

Facing uncertainties with courage builds confidence and strength, leading to personal growth, greater achievements and inner peace.

Practice: Take one step today toward something you've been avoiding out of fear. Trust that you are capable of handling the outcome.

Chapter 87: Seek Wisdom Over Knowledge

"Knowledge is knowing what to say. Wisdom is knowing whether or not to say it."
Anonymous

The Bhagavad Gita distinguishes between knowledge and wisdom. While knowledge fills the mind, wisdom nurtures the soul and guides actions.

Wisdom helps you discern right from wrong and align your life with higher truths. It leads to deeper understanding and fulfillment.

Practice: Reflect on a decision you need to make. Seek not just factual information but also consider the ethical and spiritual implications.

Chapter 88: Honesty- The Pillar of Righteous Living

"Truth is God"
Mahatma Gandhi

The Bhagvad Gita emphasizes that honesty is fundamental to living a virtuous life. Being truthful aligns us with dharma (righteousness), fosters trust, and purifies the mind.

Krishna teaches that honesty is not just about speaking the truth but living in integrity. It comprises aligning our thoughts, words, and actions with higher values.

Honesty is more than avoiding lies. it is about transparency, courage, and a commitment to moral values. By being honest, we align ourselves with the divine, develop self-respect, and foster harmony in relationships.

Practice: Be true to yourself and live in alignment with your values.

Chapter 89: Balance Material and Spiritual Life

"It is not how much we have, but how much we enjoy, that makes happiness."
Charles Spurgeon

The Bhagavad Gita emphasizes balancing material pursuits with spiritual growth. Excessive focus on either leads to instability.

A balanced life integrates worldly responsibilities with inner peace and purpose, creating true fulfillment.

Practice: Dedicate time for both work and spiritual reflection, whether through meditation, prayer, or reading spiritual texts.

Chapter 90: Trust the Process

"The best way out is always through."
Robert Frost

The Bhagavad Gita assures that every step of life's journey has a purpose. Trusting the process builds patience and perseverance.

When you trust life's flow, you face challenges with confidence and embrace outcomes with grace.

Practice: Reflect on a past hardship that led to growth. Remind yourself that your current situation will also unfold for your highest good.

Chapter 91: Faith Can Move Mountains

"Faith is taking the first step even when you don't see the whole staircase."
Martin Luther King Jr.

The Bhagavad Gita highlights the power of unwavering faith in the divine and in oneself. Faith provides strength in times of uncertainty and aligns you with higher wisdom.

Trusting in divine guidance and your abilities helps you move forward with courage, even in the face of doubt or adversity.

Practice: When faced with doubt, repeat an affirmation of trust in the divine plan, such as, "I am guided and supported in all that I do."

Chapter 92: The World is your Reflection

"What you see in others is a reflection of yourself."
Rumi

The Bhagavad Gita teaches that the world around you mirrors your inner state of mind. When you carry peace, love, and positivity within, you notice these qualities in the world and attract harmonious experiences.

When you nurture positive thoughts and emotions, the world responds in kind. Inner transformation leads to outer change. Conversely, internal negativity manifests as external conflict or dissatisfaction. It's not the world that changes, but your perception and relationship with it.

Practice: Begin each day with a positive affirmation like, "I create harmony wherever I go."

Chapter 93: Know that you are Never Alone

"The soul that walks in love shall never walk alone"
Rumi

The Bhagavad Gita assures that the divine is always with you, guiding and supporting you. You are never truly alone in your journey.

Arjuna asks,
"How do I know You're with me?"
(Bhagvad Gita 10.16)

Lord Krishna smiles,
, "Because I'm within you. I've always been. You're never alone, not for a moment."
(Bhagavad Gita 10.20)

This realization provides comfort, strength and
courage during life's challenges.

Practice: Spend a moment in prayer or meditation
today, affirming the divine presence in your life.

Chapter 94: Be Greatful for Adversity

"Adversity introduces a man to himself."
Albert Einstein

The Bhagavad Gita teaches that challenges are blessings in disguise. They refine your character and bring you closer to self-realization.

Through adversity, you develop resilience, strength, and wisdom. Each obstacle becomes a stepping stone to growth.

Practice: Reflect on a current challenge. List three ways it is helping you grow or learn, even if subtly.

Chapter 95: Be the Light in Darkness

"Darkness cannot drive out darkness; only light can do that." Martin Luther King Jr.

The Bhagavad Gita teaches that your inner light, the spark of divinity within has the power to transform darkness into hope. When faced with challenges, negativity, or despair, instead of succumbing, choose to radiate positivity and courage. This light not only illuminates your path but also inspires and uplifts those around you.

Being the light doesn't mean having all the answers; it means showing kindness, compassion, and resilience even in the face of uncertainty. It is about choosing hope over fear and love over anger.

Practice: Smile at someone who seems down or express gratitude to someone who made your day better.

Chapter 96: Resilience Through Illness

na jāyate mriyate vā kadācin
nāyaṁ bhūtvā bhavitā vā na bhūyaḥ
ajo nityaḥ śāśvato 'yaṁ purāṇo
na hanyate hanyamāne śarīre
(The Bhagvad Gita 2.20)

The Bhagavad Gita teaches the importance of remaining balanced and composed in the face of life's challenges, including the illness of a loved one. Situations of extreme difficulty, like illness, test our inner strength.

The Bhagvad Gita advises cultivating equanimity, accepting both favorable and unfavorable outcomes with the same mindset. This does not mean giving up hope or effort but letting go of anxiety and attachment to results. Inner strength arises from surrendering to the Divine and trusting in the larger cosmic plan.

Lord Krishna tells Arjuna,
"You speak of pain, Arjuna, as though it defines you. Yet
remember what you truly are cannot be touched by illness.
The soul is eternal. It neither sickens nor dies."
(The Bhagvad Gita 2.20)

In despair, Arjuna tries to explain the discomfort:
"But this suffering is real, Krishna. It wears me down, steals
my strength and will. How can I remain calm while my
body betrays me?"
(The Bhagavad Gita 1.28–1.30)

Lord Krishna elaborates:
"He who is not disturbed by pain, who stays steady in the
face of sorrow and joy alike can encompass physical pain.
Resilience, dear Arjuna, is not the absence of struggle. It is
the presence of steadiness amidst it."
(The Bhagavad Gita 2.56)

"duḥkheṣv anudvigna-manāḥ sukheṣu vigata-spṛhaḥ
vīta-rāga-bhaya-krodhaḥ sthita-dhīr munir ucyate"
(The Bhagvad Gita 2.56)

Chapter 97: Celebrate Life's Play

"To everything, there is a season, and a time for every matter under heaven."
Ecclesiastes 3:1

The Bhagavad Gita highlights that life moves in cycles, that arebirth and death, joy and sorrow. Acceptance of these cycles brings peace.

Life is a divine play (Leela). Don't take it too seriously. Embrace its joys, sorrows, and surprises with a light heart.

Understanding life's impermanence helps you face change with grace and appreciate the present moment.

Practice: Reflect on one ending or transition in your life. Find gratitude for the lessons it taught you and embrace the new cycle it brings.

Chapter 98: Trust in Karma

"You reap what you sow."
Galatians 6:7

The Bhagavad Gita teaches the law of karma: your actions create your future. Positive deeds lead to positive outcomes, while negative actions create suffering.

Understanding karma encourages mindfulness and responsibility in every choice you make.

Practice: Before taking any action today, pause and ask yourself if it aligns with your values and serves the greater good.

Chapter 99: You are Infinite

"The soul is neither born, and nor does it die."
The Bhagavad Gita

The Bhagvad Gita assures us that the soul is indestructible and eternal. Understanding this truth liberates us from the fear of death and loss. It emphasizes seeking joy in the eternal soul rather than fleeting material pursuits. True happiness comes from within.

Realizing your eternal nature brings courage and a sense of purpose. Life's trials lose their sting when seen through the lens of eternity.

You are more than your body, mind, or achievements. You are infinite, eternal, and one with the cosmos.
This inner joy remains constant, unshaken by external ups and downs. It is the essence of spiritual awakening.

Practice: Affirm "I am infinite"

Chapter 100: Life is an Illusion

"As the soul passes in this body from childhood to youth to old age, it also passes into another body at death. The wise are not deluded by this transition."
(Bhagavad Gita, Chapter 2, Verse 13)

This verse highlights the concept of maya, the illusion that binds us to the physical world and its impermanence. It reeveals that much of what we perceive is maya (illusion). True wisdom comes from seeing beyond appearances to the underlying truth.

We often identify with our bodies, roles, relationships, and material possessions, forgetting that these are temporary. The soul, which is eternal, transcends these changes.

Daivī hyeṣā guṇamayī mama māyā duratyayā
Mām eva ye prapadyante māyām etāṁ taranti te"
(Bhagvad Gita,7.14)

Lord Krishna clearly identifies the world as an illusion
that binds all beings. Only those who realize the truth of
the supreme reality can rise above it.

The illusion lies in seeing these temporary aspects as our
true identity. This attachment leads to suffering when we
face loss, change, or death. Wisdom comes from
understanding that life's transitions are like phases in a
dream real to the experiencer but ultimately not the
ultimate reality.

By recognizing life's transitions as parti of a greater
cosmic play and cultivating detachment, one can
transcend the illusion and experience true freedom.

The Bhagvad Gita underscores that life, as perceived through the material world, is transient and ever-changing. The illusion lies in identifying with the body and external circumstances, rather than recognizing the eternal nature of the soul.

When you detach from superficial judgments, life's deeper meaning becomes clear. Illusion loses its grip, and you see things as they truly are.

"Reality is merely an illusion, albeit a very persistent one."
Albert Einstein

Practice: Pause before reacting to a situation. Ask yourself, "What's the deeper reality here?" Respond with clarity and purpose.

Chapter 101: Surrender to the Divine Plan

"Let go and let God."
Anonymous

The Bhagavad Gita concludes by advocating complete surrender to the divine. Trusting the divine will brings peace, clarity, and ultimate freedom.

Lord Krishna says that every suffering, every pain and every challenge is a part of a bigger plan. Surrendering to the divine during these experiences is what shapes us for something greater.

Surrender allows you to flow with life rather than resist it, aligning you with the universe's greater plan.

Practice: At the end of the day, release all worries and intentions into the hands of the divine, trusting in the perfection of the universe.

In the final chapter (Chapter 18: Moksha Sannyasa Yoga), Arjuna continues to wrestle with uncertainty about his duty and the moral implications of war.

With deep compassion and love, Krishna gently brings his teachings to a powerful conclusion. He urges Arjuna to let go of his attachments, dissolve his ego and align his actions with the divine will.

"Sarva-dharmān parityajya māmekam śaraṇam vraja
Ahaṁ tvām sarvapāpebhyo mokṣayiṣyāmi mā śucah"
(Bhagvad Gita 18.66)

"Abandon all forms of duty and surrender completely to me. I will free you from all sins"
(Bhagvad Gita, 18.66)

Lord Krishna's final message to Arjuna is that surrendering to God doesn't mean giving up or being weak. It means letting go of pride, fear, and the need to control everything. Instead, act with love, trust and a deep sense of connection to something greater than yourself.

Epilogue: The Journey Within

As we reach the end of this journey through The Bhagavad Gita, it is not truly an end but a beginning, a stepping stone toward a more enlightened and harmonious life. The lessons within these pages are not mere philosophical musings but practical guides to transform the way we live, think, and interact with the world.

The Gita teaches us that enlightenment is not a far-off goal reserved for saints and sages; it is a state of being that anyone can achieve through self-awareness, mindful actions, and unwavering faith. By understanding these teachings and practicing them daily, we create space for peace, clarity, and purpose to emerge in our lives.

Each small step, whether it is cultivating gratitude, conquering anger, or embracing detachment, lights the path toward a more profound inner awakening. When we practice these principles consistently, they become habits, and these habits shape a life of balance, joy, and fulfillment.

Ultimately, the wisdom of The Bhagavad Gita reminds us that the answers we seek are not outside of us but within. The power to change, to find peace, and to live with purpose lies in our hands. As we apply these lessons, we uncover the eternal truth: we are not mere beings wandering through life; we are divine souls on a journey of growth, love, and self-discovery.

May these teachings inspire you to look within, practice with intention, and find enlightenment not as a distant destination but as a way of life. Let this be the beginning of your journey toward inner peace, mental stability, and a freedom that comes from letting go of ego and embracing the divine.

As The Bhagavad Gita assures us, "When the mind is pure, joy follows like a shadow that never leaves." May your journey be filled with light, love, and the serenity of knowing your true self.